Relating Is Healing

Sam Falco

Presentation by *BookLeaf Publishing*

Web: www.bookleafpub.com

E-mail: info@bookleafpub.com

ISBN: 9789363319370

First edition 2024

To my adoring husband.

ACKNOWLEDGEMENT

I would like to thank my sister and brother for their endless support and infinite love. You fill me with strength that I am forever grateful for.

PREFACE

I aspire to give comfort to all who pore over this labor of love. In this poetry book I examine enduring life's challenges amidst moments of awe. Ascend with me into life's hardships and discovering the strength I never knew laid within. Uncover the conundrum of life with me on a path back to self.

Wildflower

Wildflowers slow dance
with me into the night.
Starbursting existence
plummeting atop our dreaming souls.
The same sky we've always wished upon.
Holding all the stories ever told,
is this the closest being we may ever know?
The watcher always watching me.
The same sky it's always been,
shooting stars encompass me.
Streams gratefully pour into the sea,
ancestral wisdom welcomes you and me.
Beating hearts.
Shooting stars.
Connecting all of humanity.

Self

I've found all the flaws in you.
To the point I've forgotten my eyes are
exceptionally blue.
In the mirror I criticize you.
Love of self subdued.
Dimples in my thighs,
wrinkles surround my eyes.
Every blemish coming through.
My heart contends,
This lovely vessel carries you.

Scorn

Flatlining on the forest floor.
Shock me into something more.
Oh, I've become such a bore.
Am I the only one keeping score?
Will the shell I've become allow me to soar?
Come too close be devoured with scorn.

Attachment

Happy harmony becoming wilted
before snapping vulgar voices.
Sensual seductive keeping,
becomes tedious thoughtlessness.
We became pacified.
Craving attachment.
Losing enchantment.

Consumed

I no longer look into the eyes of my lover.
It's too hard to face the heart of another.
When I cannot feel my own heartbeat.
I hope one day our eyes meet.

Encompassed by uneasiness.
It consumed me.
The numbing process is done.
It concerned me.

How do I face the hurt inside me,
I'm no longer who I used to be.

Bloom

As true as the sun will rise,
along with the moon.
Flowers will rise and begin to bloom.
Waterfalls inherently,
the same makes you and me.
There are many things I'll never understand,
all I'll ever need is taught by this land.

Fear

Fear is the beast we all battle.
Herding our thoughts as cattle.
Reliving uncomfortable memories.
The doubt of our worth given by another.
A blink of an eye and we may wither away.

We sit in our sorrow,
wondering how to go on.
It's buried deep,
intuition and soul.

Ancestors laugh,
"How foolish they are
Bright eyes and heart
yet see no beauty at all.
Refusing the magic,
missing the call."

Silenced

I cannot save the world.
Most humans have no desire to be saved.
Not by the breaking dawn or the setting sun.
Not by the clear water creeks or within the
storms we reap.

I know the past won't set me free.
I cannot help but think of all the women before
me.
The hidden shame and secrets they retain.
Are their silenced stories leaving this sacred
world strained?

Given

What is given may break us.
Rip us open.
Witness the miracles of what we never knew.
At first, hard to admit.
To open our hearts.
one must submit.

Act

This is what happens when you don't put
yourself first.
An extra in everyone's play.
Don't you dare have a say.

This is what happens when you put yourself last.
Never escape your past.
The cycle repeats - act aghast.

Wildfire

The smoke slowly rose.
Admirable flames fueled by dead baggage
resting on the forest floor.
I also wish to burn away the difficulties I endure.
Emotions no longer useful anymore.
Liberate my mind, pacify my soul, and allow my
heart to rest.
I endlessly ask, is it all a test?

Floods

Weak and moaning.
Warped and molded.
Careful steps before imploding.
Shrouded by the damaged me.
Hazardous existences.
The worst of me.
Sobbing floods surrounding lovers.
Before, my bleeding heart asphyxiates.

Tears

Tears of our loved ones
Swell in the sea
Creating torrential hurricanes
Laving our soul
Brought to our knees

Tears of our loved one
Sweeping ocean waves
Crashing and rolling
Far and away

Tears of our loved ones
Through babbling brooks
Evaporated from our kin
Drifting into reservoirs

Tears of our loved ones
Outpouring from basins
Flooding with passion
Submerging our pain
Cascading over us
As endless memories

Phoenix

I strip down after I fall asleep.
Like a furnace in the night.
Burning off broken parts this being.
I awake bearing the vulnerable parts of me.
Risen from the ashes.
Fashioning anew me.

Morning

The morning glow peeks
soft gliding hands greet
a breach in our eyes meet
flaunting our love under sheets
no need to speak

Mind

Protector
Caretaker
Defender
Setting boundaries I don't agree to

Con
Fraud
Deceiver
Too unfamiliar to come back to

It is mine
Shape
Grow
Mend
This mind

Emotions

Our pain is our pleasure begging to be found.
We will have emotions unconfined.
Deliberately urging us to come around.

Society

Shallow thoughts
protected by radiant eyes.
Curated lies.
Caution, or society
will pick for you what to despise.